Finding You

Finding You

a guided journal of self discovery

By Elyse Hudackso

KDP

New York 2021

Finding You

INTRODUCTION

I started life on the path set out for me.
College. Career. Marriage. House. Kids.
I never gave too much thought about what I felt or what I really wanted.
I didn't really think about being present in my life and enjoying the journey.
I just sort of looked around myself and did what everyone else was doing.

Until the moment that I woke up and realized that there was limitless joy
available to those who are willing to be guided to it.

Among other practices, I began to journal every day.
Some days I wrote about a troubling situation.
Some days about something amazing that happened.
Some days about my dreams.
Some days prompted by something I read or heard.
Some days just a stream of consciousness.
But I wrote. Every day.

And I began to see how I, in my own unique way, could begin to free myself
from my bounds and live a life full of what brought me joy.

Through my journaling, I became aware of my true self.
I began to realize that negative situations were opportunities for me to let go
of limiting beliefs that held me back from experiencing joy.
I began to realize that knowing what truly lit me up inside would bring me the
ability to curate so many more joyful experiences.

*My hope is that through guided journaling, you will begin living a life in
alignment with the things that bring you joy and will begin having the
awareness to deal more calmly with the things that limit your joy.*

USING THIS JOURNAL

These pages give you with the opportunity to reflect on the many situations (past, present, and future) that tell the story of you.
The stories that reveal your true self.

You can go through the journal in order.
Or pick a prompt that calls to you in the moment.
Or you may choose to pick a page at random and surrender to exactly what you might not know you need!

You may find a natural stopping point of a prompt or just write until you fill up the pages.

You might do them all. Or leave some untouched.

Allow the prompts to inspire, guide, and transform you in your own personal way to the discovery of your truest self and your best, most beautiful life.

Date: /   /

SOMETIMES THE THING YOU DON'T
WANT TO DO
IS EXACTLY WHAT YOU NEED TO DO.

What is something you have been avoiding lately?
How might doing it really be helping you to grow?

_____

_____

_____

_____

_____

_____

_____

_____

_____

_____

_____

_____

_____

_____

_____

_____

_____

_____

_____

_____

_____

_____

_____

IF YOU GET TIRED, LEARN TO REST, NOT QUIT.

Consider something that you were once very excited about but have now given up on. How can you plan to give yourself
a break but come back to your project?

_____
_____
_____
_____
_____
_____
_____
_____
_____
_____
_____
_____
_____
_____
_____
_____
_____
_____
_____
_____
_____
_____
_____
_____
_____

BE PRESENT WITH THE WORLD AROUND YOU AND IN YOU.

Write about what you are observing
and what you are feeling.

_____

_____

_____

_____

_____

_____

_____

_____

_____

_____

_____

_____

_____

_____

_____

_____

_____

_____

_____

_____

_____

_____

_____

_____

BE WHAT YOU ARE.
NOT WHAT YOU OUGHT TO BE.

Explore one thing that you may
be doing because everyone else does or
because you have always done it that way.

_____

_____

_____

_____

_____

_____

_____

_____

_____

_____

_____

_____

_____

_____

_____

_____

_____

_____

_____

_____

_____

_____

_____

CREATIVITY INSTEAD
OF CONFORMITY

How can you bring a little more creativity into your life.
At work, in your relationships, in your dress,
in your cooking, in anything at all!

_____

_____

_____

_____

_____

_____

_____

_____

_____

_____

_____

_____

_____

_____

_____

_____

_____

_____

_____

_____

_____

_____

_____

Date: / /

BE UNAPOLOGETIC FOR HOW
YOU LIVE YOUR LIFE.

What is something that you do that goes against the grain of society?
Write yourself a love letter
celebrating your uniqueness.

_____
_____
_____
_____
_____
_____
_____
_____
_____
_____
_____
_____
_____
_____
_____
_____
_____
_____
_____
_____
_____
_____
_____
_____
_____

DO LESS WITH MORE FOCUS.

Observe something around you.
Write about it in great detail.

_____

_____

_____

_____

_____

_____

_____

_____

_____

_____

_____

_____

_____

_____

_____

_____

_____

_____

_____

_____

_____

_____

_____

_____

_____

_____

_____

RESONANCE WITH SELF
INSTEAD OF REBELLION.

Think about something that really bothers you in the world. Instead of
spending your energy in being against, think about what you are "for" instead
and figure out how you can put your energy into that.

_____
_____
_____
_____
_____
_____
_____
_____
_____
_____
_____
_____
_____
_____
_____
_____
_____
_____
_____
_____

ALL SITUATIONS ARE NEUTRAL
IT IS OUR PERSPECTIVE THAT MAKES
THEM GOOD OR BAD.

Consider a rainy day. To a bride with an outdoor wedding, it is "bad". To a farmer experiencing a drought, it is "good". In reality the situation just is. Our perspective makes it "good" or "bad".
Pick a situation in your life that feels "bad". Rewrite the situation from a perspective that makes it "good".

_____

_____

_____

_____

_____

_____

_____

_____

_____

_____

_____

_____

_____

_____

_____

_____

_____

_____

_____

_____

_____

Date: / /

TAKE THE FIRST STEP,
THE REST WILL FOLLOW.

Think about a dream that you have but
have not started journeying towards.
List at least ten tiny steps that you can take. See where they lead you!

_____

_____

_____

_____

_____

_____

_____

_____

_____

_____

_____

_____

_____

_____

_____

_____

_____

_____

_____

_____

_____

_____

_____

Date: / /

FAVOR HOPE
OVER DOUBT.

Where are you doubting yourself?
Write about what you are hoping for instead.

_____
_____
_____
_____
_____
_____
_____
_____
_____
_____
_____
_____
_____
_____
_____
_____
_____
_____
_____
_____
_____
_____
_____
_____

SEE THROUGH ILLUSION.

What if you were not seeing a challenging situation clearly?
Journal about how it could all be an illusion.

_____
_____
_____
_____
_____
_____
_____
_____
_____
_____
_____
_____
_____
_____
_____
_____
_____
_____
_____
_____
_____
_____

"NO" MIGHT JUST MEAN
"NOT NOW".

Think about something you want but have not gotten. Write about how you are actually getting it, just in a little while. What would it feel like if you knew you were getting it? How would you act? What would you do?

_____
_____
_____
_____
_____
_____
_____
_____
_____
_____
_____
_____
_____
_____
_____
_____
_____
_____
_____
_____
_____
_____
_____
_____
_____
_____
_____

THE ONLY WAY TO CHANGE
YOUR OUTER WORLD IS
TO CHANGE YOUR INNER WORLD.

List ten negative thoughts you have over and over.
Rewrite them in a more positive way.

_____

_____

_____

_____

_____

_____

_____

_____

_____

_____

_____

_____

_____

_____

_____

_____

_____

_____

_____

_____

_____

_____

_____

_____

WORDS HAVE THE POWER TO BOTH HEAL AND DESTROY. WHEN WORDS ARE BOTH TRUE AND KIND THEY CAN CHANGE OUR WORLD.

Write a love letter to yourself.

_____
_____
_____
_____
_____
_____
_____
_____
_____
_____
_____
_____
_____
_____
_____
_____
_____
_____
_____
_____
_____

YOU WILL ALWAYS BE TOO MUCH OF SOMETHING FOR SOMEONE.

What are you "too" much of? "Too" dramatic? "Too" bossy? "Too" giving?
Explore how there is no such thing as "too" much.

_____
_____
_____
_____
_____
_____
_____
_____
_____
_____
_____
_____
_____
_____
_____
_____
_____
_____
_____
_____
_____
_____
_____

Date: / /

BE BRAVE ENOUGH TO
DARE TO SEEK YOURSELF.

Write about something you really dislike about yourself. Be totally honest.

_____
_____
_____
_____
_____
_____
_____
_____
_____
_____
_____
_____
_____
_____
_____
_____
_____
_____
_____
_____
_____
_____
_____
_____
_____
_____
_____

APPRECIATE THE ORDINARY.

Fill the page with a list of everyday things and experiences that you love.

EMBRACE YOUR FULL POTENTIAL.
REFUSE TO PLAY SMALL.
DO BIG THINGS.

Write about that dream that you have
tucked away because "it will never happen".

_____

_____

_____

_____

_____

_____

_____

_____

_____

_____

_____

_____

_____

_____

_____

_____

_____

_____

_____

_____

_____

SIMPLY IMAGINE THE
END RESULT.

Write about what your life will look like in 10 years.

_____

_____

_____

_____

_____

_____

_____

_____

_____

_____

_____

_____

_____

_____

_____

_____

_____

_____

_____

_____

_____

_____

_____

_____

IF YOU CAN'T WAIT TO HAVE IT,
YOU MIGHT WANT IT FOR
THE WRONG REASONS.

Name something you are impatient to have. Explore why you want it so badly
that you wish you did not have to wait.

_____

_____

_____

_____

_____

_____

_____

_____

_____

_____

_____

_____

_____

_____

_____

_____

_____

_____

_____

IT'S NOT ABOUT FORCING,
IT'S ABOUT ALIGNING.

What are you trying to force in your life?
What is the feeling that you are really trying to achieve?
How can you achieve that with more ease?

_____

_____

_____

_____

_____

_____

_____

_____

_____

_____

_____

_____

_____

_____

_____

_____

_____

_____

_____

_____

_____

LIFE REQUIRES BOTH
ACCEPTANCE AND ACTION.

Picture a challenging situation in your life. How can you accept it? And how can you take action to move in a more positive direction?

_____

_____

_____

_____

_____

_____

_____

_____

_____

_____

_____

_____

_____

_____

_____

_____

_____

_____

_____

_____

_____

_____

_____

_____

_____

_____

IF YOU WANT TO BE HAPPY,
MAKE OTHERS HAPPY.

Write about something really nice you did for someone.
Explore how it made you feel.

_____
_____
_____
_____
_____
_____
_____
_____
_____
_____
_____
_____
_____
_____
_____
_____
_____
_____
_____
_____
_____
_____
_____
_____
_____
_____
_____

IT IS IMPORTANT TO UNDERSTAND
THE DIFFERENCE BETWEEN DISCOMFORT AND
DISINTEREST.

Think about something that you think you want to do but just aren't doing.
Explore the difference between discomfort and disinterest.

_____
_____
_____
_____
_____
_____
_____
_____
_____
_____
_____
_____
_____
_____
_____
_____
_____
_____
_____
_____
_____
_____
_____

IT IS OKAY TO HAVE A LIFE THAT OTHERS JUST DON'T UNDERSTAND.

Write about something you do that brings you great joy but that some people in your life find unnecessary.

_____
_____
_____
_____
_____
_____
_____
_____
_____
_____
_____
_____
_____
_____
_____
_____
_____
_____
_____
_____
_____

Date: / /

SITTING WITH YOUR PAIN
TRANSFORMS IT INTO WISDOM.

Think of a struggle you are having right now.
What could it be teaching you?

_____
_____
_____
_____
_____
_____
_____
_____
_____
_____
_____
_____
_____
_____
_____
_____
_____
_____
_____
_____
_____
_____
_____

INNER PEACE IS ALWAYS
AN OPTION.

List the ways you can deal
with negative emotions.

_____

_____

_____

_____

_____

_____

_____

_____

_____

_____

_____

_____

_____

_____

_____

_____

_____

_____

_____

_____

_____

_____

_____

YOUR GREAT CONTRIBUTION TO HUMANITY REQUIRES YOU FIRST TO HAVE THIS EXPERIENCE.

In what ways can the lessons of a difficult experience you are having right now help you to make a greater contribution to humanity?

_____
_____
_____
_____
_____
_____
_____
_____
_____
_____
_____
_____
_____
_____
_____
_____
_____
_____
_____
_____
_____
_____
_____
_____

IT IS OKAY TO NOT KNOW
HOW THIS BENEFITS YOU YET.

Journal about how you can let go of trying to figure out why something is happening to you.

_____
_____
_____
_____
_____
_____
_____
_____
_____
_____
_____
_____
_____
_____
_____
_____
_____
_____
_____
_____
_____
_____
_____
_____
_____

COMPARISON IS SIMPLY THE LACK OF FAITH THAT YOUR PATH IS THE ONE THAT WILL BRING YOU THE GREATEST HAPPINESS

Where are you comparing yourself to someone else? Write the story of how your own experience, not theirs, is going to bring you your greatest happiness.

_____

_____

_____

_____

_____

_____

_____

_____

_____

_____

_____

_____

_____

_____

_____

_____

_____

_____

_____

_____

_____

_____

_____

_____

_____

_____

_____

THE OUTCOME IS THE COMBINATION OF THE EVENT AND YOUR REACTION.

Write about how a recent reaction could have been different and rewrite the outcome based on a new, more positive reaction.

_____
_____
_____
_____
_____
_____
_____
_____
_____
_____
_____
_____
_____
_____
_____
_____
_____
_____
_____
_____
_____
_____
_____
_____
_____

BE GRATEFUL FOR THE THINGS THAT TEST US FOR THEY HELP US GROW.

How did you grow out of a recent
difficult situation?

_____
_____
_____
_____
_____
_____
_____
_____
_____
_____
_____
_____
_____
_____
_____
_____
_____
_____
_____
_____
_____
_____
_____

BE THE REASON
SOMEONE SMILES TODAY.

Fill the page with ways to make the people in your life smile today. Do them all!

_____
_____
_____
_____
_____
_____
_____
_____
_____
_____
_____
_____
_____
_____
_____
_____
_____
_____
_____
_____
_____
_____

UNLEARN EVERYTHING
AND FREE YOUR MIND.

What is something you wish
you could unlearn?

_____

_____

_____

_____

_____

_____

_____

_____

_____

_____

_____

_____

_____

_____

_____

_____

_____

_____

_____

_____

_____

_____

_____

Date: / /

ASK YOURSELF IF WHAT YOU ARE DOING TODAY IS GETTING YOU CLOSER TO WHERE YOU WANT TO BE TOMORROW.

What are you spending a lot of your time on right now? What skills and character traits is it helping you build?

_____

_____

_____

_____

_____

_____

_____

_____

_____

_____

_____

_____

_____

_____

_____

_____

_____

_____

_____

_____

_____

_____

_____

_____

YOU KNOW THE TRUTH
BY THE WAY IT FEELS.

Where are you talking yourself out of something you know
is true because you don't want it to be?

_____

_____

_____

_____

_____

_____

_____

_____

_____

_____

_____

_____

_____

_____

_____

_____

_____

_____

_____

_____

_____

THINK ABOUT YOUR LEGACY FOR YOU ARE WRITING IT EVERY DAY.

Put yourself ahead 20 years. What impact will you have
wanted to have on humanity, big or small!

_____
_____
_____
_____
_____
_____
_____
_____
_____
_____
_____
_____
_____
_____
_____
_____
_____
_____
_____
_____
_____
_____
_____
_____

ALWAYS BE A LITTLE
KINDER THAN NECESSARY.

Write about the last really kind thing you did for someone in your life.

BELIEVE YOU CAN AND
YOU'RE HALFWAY THERE.

Think about something you want to accomplish. Write a review of your finished work.

_____
_____
_____
_____
_____
_____
_____
_____
_____
_____
_____
_____
_____
_____
_____
_____
_____
_____
_____
_____
_____
_____
_____
_____
_____

WHEN "AND" IS POSSIBLE,
WHY CHOOSE "OR"?

What is a decision you are making right now? Explore how you don't have to
decide between the two, but can actually have both.

_____
_____
_____
_____
_____
_____
_____
_____
_____
_____
_____
_____
_____
_____
_____
_____
_____
_____
_____
_____
_____
_____
_____
_____
_____
_____
_____
_____
_____

Date: / /

YOU ARE IN THE PROCESS OF BECOMING THE BEST VERSION OR YOURSELF.

Describe the very best version of you.

_____
_____
_____
_____
_____
_____
_____
_____
_____
_____
_____
_____
_____
_____
_____
_____
_____
_____
_____
_____
_____
_____
_____
_____
_____

ASK YOURSELF,
"WHAT ELSE COULD THIS MEAN?".

Think of something that has made you feel "less than" recently.
What else could it have meant?

_____

_____

_____

_____

_____

_____

_____

_____

_____

_____

_____

_____

_____

_____

_____

_____

_____

_____

_____

_____

_____

_____

_____

_____

_____

LET YOUR DREAMS BE BIGGER
THAN YOUR FEARS.

List all the things that are holding you back from pursuing a dream?
Cross them out and write why you can do it.

_____
_____
_____
_____
_____
_____
_____
_____
_____
_____
_____
_____
_____
_____
_____
_____
_____
_____
_____
_____
_____
_____
_____

DWELL IN POSSIBILITY.

Fill the page with a list of things you could do today.

_____
_____
_____
_____
_____
_____
_____
_____
_____
_____
_____
_____
_____
_____
_____
_____
_____
_____
_____
_____
_____
_____
_____
_____
_____
_____
_____

A LONGING TO CREATE
IS TRUE VITALITY.

Think of something you would like to create. Describe it in great detail.

_____
_____
_____
_____
_____
_____
_____
_____
_____
_____
_____
_____
_____
_____
_____
_____
_____
_____
_____
_____
_____
_____
_____

YOU MAY NOT BE THERE YET,
BUT YOU ARE CLOSER
THAN YOU WERE YESTERDAY.

Write about the progress you are making on a project in your life.
Reflect on where you started and how far you have come.

_____

_____

_____

_____

_____

_____

_____

_____

_____

_____

_____

_____

_____

_____

_____

_____

_____

_____

_____

_____

_____

_____

_____

_____

ALLOW THE UPSET
TO EXHALE.

Rant about something that is bothering you.
Let it all out.

_____

_____

_____

_____

_____

_____

_____

_____

_____

_____

_____

_____

_____

_____

_____

_____

_____

_____

_____

_____

_____

_____

_____

_____

THE ONLY RESPONSE TO
PAIN IS COMPASSION.

Think of someone who is bothering you. Explore what pain they might be in
and how can you show compassion.

_____
_____
_____
_____
_____
_____
_____
_____
_____
_____
_____
_____
_____
_____
_____
_____
_____
_____
_____
_____
_____
_____

CELEBRATE YOURSELF
FOR NO REASON AT ALL

Use the space below to plan a celebration
day for yourself. Then do it!

_____

_____

_____

_____

_____

_____

_____

_____

_____

_____

_____

_____

_____

_____

_____

_____

_____

_____

_____

_____

_____

_____

BETTER TO BE CLUMSY IN OUR EARNESTNESS THAN COMPLICIT IN OUR SILENCE.

Where are you not doing something because you don't know what to do?
Journal about a few ways you might be able to help..

_____
_____
_____
_____
_____
_____
_____
_____
_____
_____
_____
_____
_____
_____
_____
_____
_____
_____
_____
_____
_____
_____
_____

Date: / /

THE THINGS THAT FRIGHTEN YOU ARE THE THINGS THAT OWN YOUR POWER.

Explore one thing that frightens you and how it is holding you back.

_____

_____

_____

_____

_____

_____

_____

_____

_____

_____

_____

_____

_____

_____

_____

_____

_____

_____

_____

_____

_____

_____

_____

WHAT GOT YOU HERE
WON'T GET YOU THERE.

Where do you want to go? What is one thing you can start doing differently to
get you closer?

_____

_____

_____

_____

_____

_____

_____

_____

_____

_____

_____

_____

_____

_____

_____

_____

_____

_____

_____

_____

_____

_____

_____

LEARN TO
STOP THE SHOW.

Where can you go all out today? Where could you be a total superstar?

_____

_____

_____

_____

_____

_____

_____

_____

_____

_____

_____

_____

_____

_____

_____

_____

_____

_____

_____

_____

_____

_____

_____

_____

_____

_____

_____

IF THIS WERE TO LAST FOREVER, HOW WOULD YOU FIND PEACE OF MIND?

Imagine that a difficult situation in your life will not go away.
How will you need to change your mindset to have peace?

_____
_____
_____
_____
_____
_____
_____
_____
_____
_____
_____
_____
_____
_____
_____
_____
_____
_____
_____
_____
_____
_____

RESPOND WITH AWARENESS,
NOT ATTACHMENT

Journal about how you recently responded to someone. Were you observing
and learning? Or trying to get to a certain outcome?

_____

_____

_____

_____

_____

_____

_____

_____

_____

_____

_____

_____

_____

_____

_____

_____

_____

_____

_____

_____

_____

YOUR COMMITMENT TO YOUR GOAL SHOULD NOT BE CONTINGENT
UPON YOUR ABILITY TO ATTAIN IT.

Write about something you would love to do if you were not worried about wasting your time.

WITH TIME
THERE IS CLARITY.

Write about an event from your past
that looks very different to you now than when it was happening.

_____
_____
_____
_____
_____
_____
_____
_____
_____
_____
_____
_____
_____
_____
_____
_____
_____
_____
_____
_____
_____
_____
_____
_____

WE CAN PLANT SEEDS BUT WE CANNOT FORCE THEM TO GROW.

Is there someone in your life you are trying to change?
Explore how you can inspire instead of change.

_____
_____
_____
_____
_____
_____
_____
_____
_____
_____
_____
_____
_____
_____
_____
_____
_____
_____
_____
_____
_____
_____
_____
_____
_____
_____

REMEMBER, EVERYTHING
IS TEMPORARY.

Take a challenging situation you are having.
Write about what it will look like in three years.

_____

_____

_____

_____

_____

_____

_____

_____

_____

_____

_____

_____

_____

_____

_____

_____

_____

_____

_____

_____

_____

_____

HOLD THE VISION.
TRUST THE PROCESS.

Clearly describe your vision for something you want.

_____

_____

_____

_____

_____

_____

_____

_____

_____

_____

_____

_____

_____

_____

_____

_____

_____

_____

_____

_____

_____

_____

EVERY FAILURE IS A
STEP CLOSER TO SUCCESS.

Describe a great failure that you had. How did it contribute to a later success?

_____
_____
_____
_____
_____
_____
_____
_____
_____
_____
_____
_____
_____
_____
_____
_____
_____
_____
_____
_____
_____
_____
_____

THE FEARS YOU DON'T FACE
BECOME YOUR REGRETS.

Journal about something you regret not doing and the fear that stopped you from doing it. How can you face that fear now?

_____

_____

_____

_____

_____

_____

_____

_____

_____

_____

_____

_____

_____

_____

_____

_____

_____

_____

_____

_____

_____

_____

_____

_____

_____

_____

Date: / /

MY VALUES:
KINDNESS. AUTHENTICITY. MINDFULNESS.
DETERMINATION. JOY.

Make a list of the characteristics you value.
Brainstorm the characteristics of people you admire then look for similarities
to come up with your list.

_____

_____

_____

_____

_____

_____

_____

_____

_____

_____

_____

_____

_____

_____

_____

_____

_____

_____

_____

_____

WHAT YOU APPRECIATE, APPRECIATES.

Fill the page with a list of things about yourself that you really love.

_____

_____

_____

_____

_____

_____

_____

_____

_____

_____

_____

_____

_____

_____

_____

_____

_____

_____

_____

_____

_____

_____

_____

_____

_____

THE MOST GENEROUS PERSON
IN THE ROOM ALWAYS WINS.

Write a thank you note to yourself for something generous you recently did.

_____

_____

_____

_____

_____

_____

_____

_____

_____

_____

_____

_____

_____

_____

_____

_____

_____

_____

_____

_____

_____

_____

_____

YOU CAN EITHER FIT IN OR
STAND OUT. NOT BOTH.

Journal about one way that you can really stand out today.

_____
_____
_____
_____
_____
_____
_____
_____
_____
_____
_____
_____
_____
_____
_____
_____
_____
_____
_____
_____
_____
_____

IF YOU ARE GROWING,
YOU ARE WINNING.

Recount a time in your life when you went through a huge growth experience
and end with how it was a huge win!.

_____

_____

_____

_____

_____

_____

_____

_____

_____

_____

_____

_____

_____

_____

_____

_____

_____

_____

_____

_____

IMAGINE THAT EVERY PERSON IN THE WORLD IS ENLIGHTENED BUT YOU.

Write about your day, but imagine each interaction you had as if that person were a teacher here to teach you patience, tolerance, and love.

_____
_____
_____
_____
_____
_____
_____
_____
_____
_____
_____
_____
_____
_____
_____
_____
_____
_____
_____
_____

YOUR BELIEF IS
NOT MY TRUTH.

What is a very common belief that just does not resonate with you?
What is your actual truth?

_____
_____
_____
_____
_____
_____
_____
_____
_____
_____
_____
_____
_____
_____
_____
_____
_____
_____
_____
_____
_____
_____

YOU ARE ALWAYS ACTING OUT OF EITHER LOVE OR FEAR. ALWAYS ACT OUT OF LOVE.

Think of a decision you are contemplating. Which choice do you love and which choice helps you avoid something scary?

_____

_____

_____

_____

_____

_____

_____

_____

_____

_____

_____

_____

_____

_____

_____

_____

_____

_____

_____

_____

_____

_____

_____

IN EVERY MOMENT AS A HUMAN
YOU EITHER GROW OR SHRINK.

Journal about the last interaction you had. In what ways did you blossom and
in what ways did you get smaller?

_____

_____

_____

_____

_____

_____

_____

_____

_____

_____

_____

_____

_____

_____

_____

_____

_____

_____

_____

_____

_____

_____

_____

_____

FORGIVENESS IS THE DECISION TO LET GO OF THE DESIRE FOR
REVENGE OR ILL WILL.

Explore a place in your life where
you would like to forgive. Write out how you could go about doing that.

_____
_____
_____
_____
_____
_____
_____
_____
_____
_____
_____
_____
_____
_____
_____
_____
_____
_____
_____
_____
_____
_____
_____
_____

WHERE YOU STUMBLE,
THERE'S YOUR TREASURE.

Where are you struggling right now?
Write out how this is actually benefiting your growth
and will make you happier in the end.

_____

_____

_____

_____

_____

_____

_____

_____

_____

_____

_____

_____

_____

_____

_____

_____

_____

_____

_____

_____

_____

_____

_____

WHEN YOU WANT SOMETHING, BE ALL IN WITH YOUR MIND, BODY, AND SOUL.

Think about something you would really love to have. What actions can you take with your mind, with your body, and with your soul in the direction of your desire.

_____

_____

_____

_____

_____

_____

_____

_____

_____

_____

_____

_____

_____

_____

_____

_____

_____

_____

_____

_____

_____

_____

GREAT THINGS NEVER
COME FROM COMFORT ZONES.

Journal about one way you can get out of your comfort zone.

_____

_____

_____

_____

_____

_____

_____

_____

_____

_____

_____

_____

_____

_____

_____

_____

_____

_____

_____

_____

_____

_____

_____

Date: / /

CONTEMPLATION IS THE
HIGHEST FORM OF ACTIVITY.

Just write without any purpose and see what comes up for you.

WHEN WE ARE OUT OF TOUCH
WITH OURSELVES WE
ARE EASILY MISLED.

Write about a time when you did not hold true to your values, or did not know what your values were, and you did something that was not of your best self.

_____

_____

_____

_____

_____

_____

_____

_____

_____

_____

_____

_____

_____

_____

_____

_____

_____

_____

_____

_____

_____

_____

_____

_____

THE ONLY PERSON YOU ARE
DESTINED TO BECOME
IS THE ONE YOU DECIDE TO BE.

Paint a picture of who you want to be in ten years.
Act like that person today!

_____
_____
_____
_____
_____
_____
_____
_____
_____
_____
_____
_____
_____
_____
_____
_____
_____
_____
_____
_____
_____
_____
_____
_____

JUDGEMENT.
IT'S WHAT WE DO WHEN WE DON'T UNDERSTAND.

Contemplate someone in your life
you are judging.

_____
_____
_____
_____
_____
_____
_____
_____
_____
_____
_____
_____
_____
_____
_____
_____
_____
_____
_____
_____

TREAT EACH DAY AS IF
IT IS A MINIATURE LIFETIME.

Think about what you have planned for the upcoming day. How can you make each activity meaningful and memorable?

_____
_____
_____
_____
_____
_____
_____
_____
_____
_____
_____
_____
_____
_____
_____
_____
_____
_____
_____
_____
_____
_____

ASK FOR WHAT YOU WANT.
THEN LET GO OF HOW IT COMES TO YOU.

Explore something that you really want until you hit upon the "feeling" you are looking for. Start focusing on the "feeling" instead of the "thing".

_____

_____

_____

_____

_____

_____

_____

_____

_____

_____

_____

_____

_____

_____

_____

_____

_____

_____

_____

_____

THINGS THAT EXCITE YOU ARE NOT RANDOM.
THEY ARE CONNECTED TO YOUR PURPOSE.
FOLLOW THEM.

Write about something that really excites you.
How can you bring more of that into your life?

_____

_____

_____

_____

_____

_____

_____

_____

_____

_____

_____

_____

_____

_____

_____

_____

_____

_____

_____

_____

_____

_____

Date: / /

SAY 'YES' TO OPPORTUNITIES THAT
ALIGN WITH YOUR SOUL

When was the last time you said 'yes'?

_____
_____
_____
_____
_____
_____
_____
_____
_____
_____
_____
_____
_____
_____
_____
_____
_____
_____
_____
_____
_____
_____
_____
_____
_____

Date: / /

BRAVERY IS THE
ANTIDOTE TO REGRET.

Where is a place in your life that you can be a little braver than you feel?

_____

_____

_____

_____

_____

_____

_____

_____

_____

_____

_____

_____

_____

_____

_____

_____

_____

_____

_____

_____

_____

_____

_____

_____

SOMETIMES YOU HAVE TO FORGET WHAT YOU THINK AND REMEMBER WHAT YOU DESERVE.

Where do you feel a sense of lack? Rewrite the story in a way that celebrates how much you deserve what you are lacking.

_____
_____
_____
_____
_____
_____
_____
_____
_____
_____
_____
_____
_____
_____
_____
_____
_____
_____
_____
_____

STOP TALKING ABOUT YOUR PROBLEMS.
START TALKING ABOUT YOUR JOYS.

Fill the page with a list of things that make you crazy happy.

_____
_____
_____
_____
_____
_____
_____
_____
_____
_____
_____
_____
_____
_____
_____
_____
_____
_____
_____
_____

Date: / /

THE JOURNEY ISN'T ABOUT
BECOMING A DIFFERENT PERSON
BUT LOVING WHO YOU ARE RIGHT NOW.

Journal about all the things you love about yourself

_____
_____
_____
_____
_____
_____
_____
_____
_____
_____
_____
_____
_____
_____
_____
_____
_____
_____
_____
_____
_____
_____

Date: / /

THAT WHICH WE DO NOT BRING TO CONSCIOUSNESS APPEARS LATER IN OUR LIVES AS FATE.

What is something you are not dealing with?
How might ignoring it negatively
impact you later?

_____
_____
_____
_____
_____
_____
_____
_____
_____
_____
_____
_____
_____
_____
_____
_____
_____
_____
_____
_____
_____
_____
_____
_____

IF YOU DON'T MAKE MISTAKES, YOU ARE NOT LEARNING.

Journal about a mistake you made and what you learned from it.

CRISIS PRECEDES TRANSFORMATION.

Journal about a time of crisis
and how it transformed you.

_____
_____
_____
_____
_____
_____
_____
_____
_____
_____
_____
_____
_____
_____
_____
_____
_____
_____
_____
_____
_____
_____

Date: / /

ALWAYS LEAVE A LITTLE
SPARKLE WHEREVER YOU GO.

What are some things you can do today to make the day a little brighter?.

_____
_____
_____
_____
_____
_____
_____
_____
_____
_____
_____
_____
_____
_____
_____
_____
_____
_____
_____
_____
_____
_____

EVERYONE AND EVERYTHING IS A TEACHER, UNLESS YOU ARE A POOR STUDENT.

Write about something in your life that is showing up as a teacher right now.
What are you learning?

_____

_____

_____

_____

_____

_____

_____

_____

_____

_____

_____

_____

_____

_____

_____

_____

_____

_____

_____

_____

_____

WHAT NEEDS TO HAPPEN
FOR THIS TO BE A GREAT DAY?

Make a list of all the things that could happen to make today great.

_____

_____

_____

_____

_____

_____

_____

_____

_____

_____

_____

_____

_____

_____

_____

_____

_____

_____

_____

_____

_____

_____

_____

_____

IF YOU HAVE THE CHANCE TO MAKE PEOPLE HAPPY, JUST DO IT.

Think back over the past week. What are some things you could have done just to make someone else happy?

_____

_____

_____

_____

_____

_____

_____

_____

_____

_____

_____

_____

_____

_____

_____

_____

_____

_____

_____

_____

_____

TRUST YOUR INNER
KNOWING IN ALL SITUATION.

Journal about a time when
you followed your intuition.

_____
_____
_____
_____
_____
_____
_____
_____
_____
_____
_____
_____
_____
_____
_____
_____
_____
_____
_____
_____
_____
_____
_____
_____
_____

GO TO THE EDGE OF YOUR LIMITS BECAUSE THAT IS HOW YOUR LIMITS EXPAND.

Explore an area of your life where you can stretch yourself to go a little past comfortable.

_____

_____

_____

_____

_____

_____

_____

_____

_____

_____

_____

_____

_____

_____

_____

_____

_____

_____

_____

_____

_____

_____

_____

Date: / /

GIVE YOURSELF SOME CREDIT
FOR HOW FAR YOU'VE COME.

Think back five years. Journal about how you have grown and transformed.

_____
_____
_____
_____
_____
_____
_____
_____
_____
_____
_____
_____
_____
_____
_____
_____
_____
_____
_____
_____
_____
_____

LOVE AND FEAR CANNOT COEXIST.

Where are you having some negative feelings?
Find lots of positive things to write about the situation instead.

_____
_____
_____
_____
_____
_____
_____
_____
_____
_____
_____
_____
_____
_____
_____
_____
_____
_____
_____
_____
_____
_____
_____

WHEN SOMETHING DOESN'T GO YOUR WAY, THINK "PLOT TWIST".

Plot twists are necessary to keep a story interesting.
Write about one of your real-life plot twists.

_____
_____
_____
_____
_____
_____
_____
_____
_____
_____
_____
_____
_____
_____
_____
_____
_____
_____
_____
_____
_____
_____
_____
_____
_____
_____

Date: / /

BECOME FEROCIOUS IN YOUR QUEST FOR GREATNESS.

What is something you would like to be great at?
How can you put more excitement and energy there?

_____
_____
_____
_____
_____
_____
_____
_____
_____
_____
_____
_____
_____
_____
_____
_____
_____
_____
_____
_____
_____

IT IS EASY TO TALK OF
HOW THINGS SHOULD BE. IT TAKES TOUGHNESS TO
ACCEPT HOW THEY ARE.

Explore where you are putting energy into how you wish things were and then
explore how you can accept how they actually are.

_____

_____

_____

_____

_____

_____

_____

_____

_____

_____

_____

_____

_____

_____

_____

_____

_____

_____

_____

_____

_____

_____

_____

_____

YOU BEING DIFFERENT SCARES
OTHER PEOPLE.

Where have changes you have made in yourself
been met by resistance by others?

_____
_____
_____
_____
_____
_____
_____
_____
_____
_____
_____
_____
_____
_____
_____
_____
_____
_____
_____
_____
_____
_____
_____
_____

SAY 'YES" WHERE YOU
WOULD NORMALLY SAY 'NO'.

Make a list of all the things you tend to say "no" to. Explore how you will say "yes" the next time.

_____

_____

_____

_____

_____

_____

_____

_____

_____

_____

_____

_____

_____

_____

_____

_____

_____

_____

_____

_____

_____

_____

_____

_____

_____

WE MUST PUT ENERGY AND EFFORT INTO ANYTHING WE WISH TO CHANGE.

What is one thing you would like to change? Fill the page with ideas on things you could do to head in that direction.

_____

_____

_____

_____

_____

_____

_____

_____

_____

_____

_____

_____

_____

_____

_____

_____

_____

_____

_____

_____

_____

_____

_____

_____

Date: / /

THE FEARS WE DON'T
FACE BECOME OUR LIMITS.

What is a fear that you are not facing? In what ways is it holding you back
from being your greatest self?

_____
_____
_____
_____
_____
_____
_____
_____
_____
_____
_____
_____
_____
_____
_____
_____
_____
_____
_____
_____
_____
_____

LOVE THINGS AS
THEY ARE.

How can you fall in love with something in your life
that you currently find annoying?

_____
_____
_____
_____
_____
_____
_____
_____
_____
_____
_____
_____
_____
_____
_____
_____
_____
_____
_____
_____
_____
_____
_____
_____

SOMETIME THE SMALLEST
STEP IN THE RIGHT DIRECTION BECOMES THE BIGGEST
STEP OF YOUR LIFE.

Fill the page with small steps you can take in the direction of a dream.

_____

_____

_____

_____

_____

_____

_____

_____

_____

_____

_____

_____

_____

_____

_____

_____

_____

_____

_____

_____

_____

_____

_____

_____

_____

WHAT'S COMING IS BETTER
THAN WHAT'S GONE.

Take time to mourn something that you have lost. Then give yourself a
moment to smile about what is coming.

_____
_____
_____
_____
_____
_____
_____
_____
_____
_____
_____
_____
_____
_____
_____
_____
_____
_____
_____
_____
_____
_____
_____
_____
_____

WHAT PEOPLE THINK OF YOU MUST BE PUT ASIDE FOR PEACE.

Journal about an opinion of you that is bothering you until you are ready to let it go.

_____

_____

_____

_____

_____

_____

_____

_____

_____

_____

_____

_____

_____

_____

_____

_____

_____

_____

_____

_____

_____

_____

THE CLOSER WE GET TO OUR AUTHENTIC SELF THE BRIGHTER WE SHINE.

Explore how you have begun to shine more brightly as you have traveled the path of self-discovery.

ATTITUDE IS THE DIFFERENCE BETWEEN AN ORDEAL AND AN ADVENTURE.

Think about something on the horizon that you don't want to do and write about how you can change your attitude.

_____

_____

_____

_____

_____

_____

_____

_____

_____

_____

_____

_____

_____

_____

_____

_____

_____

_____

_____

_____

_____

_____

_____

EVERY REACTION IS
A CHOICE.

Think of a situation where you were not your best self.
How could you have reacted differently?

_____
_____
_____
_____
_____
_____
_____
_____
_____
_____
_____
_____
_____
_____
_____
_____
_____
_____
_____
_____
_____
_____
_____
_____
_____

Date: / /

SLOW DOWN AND
NOTICE.

Make a list of all the things you are observing right now about yourself.

_____
_____
_____
_____
_____
_____
_____
_____
_____
_____
_____
_____
_____
_____
_____
_____
_____
_____
_____
_____
_____
_____
_____

Date: / /

YOUR INNER PEACE IS
YOUR POWER.

Journal about ways you can find calm in situations that
normally disrupt your peace.

_____
_____
_____
_____
_____
_____
_____
_____
_____
_____
_____
_____
_____
_____
_____
_____
_____
_____
_____
_____
_____
_____
_____
_____
_____
_____
_____

EXPECT TO SUCCEED.

Write a story about a
future success.

_____

_____

_____

_____

_____

_____

_____

_____

_____

_____

_____

_____

_____

_____

_____

_____

_____

_____

_____

_____

Date: / /

BE SURE YOUR
THINKING IS EMPOWERING.

List every thought you have today that is not
empowering you to be your greatest self.

_____
_____
_____
_____
_____
_____
_____
_____
_____
_____
_____
_____
_____
_____
_____
_____
_____
_____
_____

PUT YOURSELF IN A
POSITION TO RECEIVE.

Journal about a place in your life that you need to make room for something better. What do you need to eliminate?

_____
_____
_____
_____
_____
_____
_____
_____
_____
_____
_____
_____
_____
_____
_____
_____
_____
_____
_____
_____
_____
_____
_____

Date: / /

MAKE TIME
TO LISTEN.

Write down all the thoughts in your head for the next few minutes.

_____

_____

_____

_____

_____

_____

_____

_____

_____

_____

_____

_____

_____

_____

_____

_____

_____

_____

_____

_____

_____

_____